EXPLORE BIOMES

FOREST BIOMES

BY CLARA MacCARALD

Kids Core
An Imprint of Abdo Publishing
abdobooks.com

abdobooks.com

Published by Abdo Publishing, a division of ABDO, PO Box 398166, Minneapolis, Minnesota 55439.

Printed in the United States of America, North Mankato, Minnesota.
052023
092023

THIS BOOK CONTAINS
RECYCLED MATERIALS

Cover Photo: Shutterstock Images
Interior Photos: Shutterstock Images, 4–5, 26, 28 (squirrel, bear, fox), 29 (deer); Ondrej Prosicky/Shutterstock Images, 7; Gregory G. Dimijian, M.D./Science Source, 8; Claes Touber/iStockphoto, 10–11; Gabi Wolf/Shutterstock Images, 13; Joanne Hedger/Moment/Getty Images, 15; Stefan Gottermann/Shutterstock Images, 16; Sergey Uryadnikov/Shutterstock Images, 18–19; Michael Tatman/iStockphoto, 21; Jared Lloyd/Moment/Getty Images, 23; Mircea Costina/Shutterstock Images, 25; Sketched Images/Shutterstock Images, 28–29; VectorShow/Shutterstock Images, 29 (beetle, ant)

Editor: Angela Lim
Series Designer: Ryan Gale

Library of Congress Control Number: 2022949087

Publisher's Cataloging-in-Publication Data

Names: MacCarald, Clara, author.
Title: Forest biomes / by Clara MacCarald
Description: Minneapolis, Minnesota: Abdo Publishing Company, 2024 | Series: Explore biomes | Includes online resources and index.
Identifiers: ISBN 9781098291082 (lib. bdg.) | ISBN 9781098277260 (ebook)
Subjects: LCSH: Forests and forestry--Juvenile literature. | Biotic communities--Juvenile literature. | Habitats--Juvenile literature. | Life zones--Juvenile literature. | Forest animals--Juvenile literature. | Forest plants--Juvenile literature. | Forest ecology--Juvenile literature.
Classification: DDC 577--dc23

CONTENTS

CHAPTER 1
A Fall Feast 4

CHAPTER 2
What Makes a Forest? 10

CHAPTER 3
A Forest Community 18

Explore the Biome 28
Glossary 30
Online Resources 31
Learn More 31
Index 32
About the Author 32

Squirrels have a wide diet. They eat nuts, fruits, insects, and more.

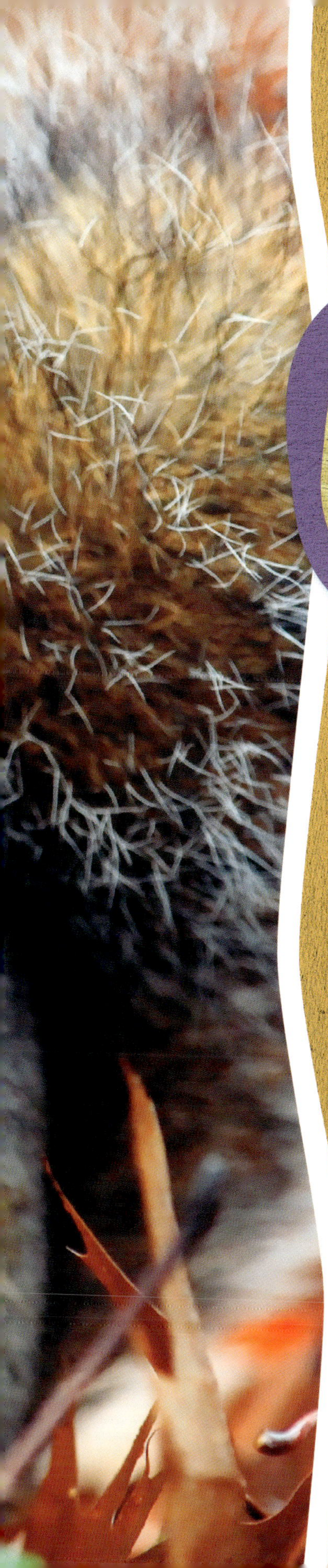

CHAPTER 1

A FALL FEAST

It is fall in the forest. Oak and hickory trees form the top layer of the forest. Their green leaves have started turning red and gold.

Leaves cover the forest floor. A gray squirrel leaps through them. It is looking for acorns.

Oak trees drop these nuts in the fall. The squirrel needs to gather as many acorns as it can. It will bury them somewhere safe. The stored nuts will help the squirrel survive the winter.

The squirrel spots the scaly cap of an acorn. It runs over to the nut. It uses its mouth to pick up the acorn.

The Redwood Forest

Redwood forests grow mostly in California near the coast. Redwood trees are the tallest type of tree in the world. They can be more than 360 feet (110 m) tall. Redwoods can live for 2,000 years.

Red-tailed hawks can spot prey from high in the air.

Suddenly a shadow swoops over the squirrel. It's a red-tailed hawk! The hawk's claws just miss the squirrel.

The squirrel drops its acorn in fear. It races up the trunk of an oak tree. It looks down at the **predator**. The squirrel jerks its fluffy tail back and forth. It also warns other squirrels.

Giant sequoia forests can have trees that are more than 300 feet (91 m) tall.

The squirrel barks an alarm to signal danger. The hawk takes off to search for new **prey**.

Forest Biomes

A biome includes the plants and animals that live in a particular region. It also includes nonliving things. Forest biomes have many trees. Squirrels and hawks are forest animals. Soil and air are nonliving parts of the forest.

Forests grow all around the world. The kinds of plants and animals that live in a forest depend on the **climate**. Together, forest biomes cover about one-third of Earth's land.

Explore Online

Visit the website below. Does it give any new information about gray squirrels that wasn't in Chapter One?

Eastern Gray Squirrel

abdocorelibrary.com/forest-biomes

Mushrooms that grow on the forest floor help improve soil health.

CHAPTER 2

WHAT MAKES A FOREST?

Forests have several layers. The bottom layer is the forest floor. It is made up of soil. It also includes animal waste and plant waste, such as leaves. Grasses and flowers form the next layer, which is called the herb layer. Then comes the shrub layer.

Young and short trees form the understory layer. Tall trees make up the canopy. The tallest trees rise into the emergent layer.

There are three main types of forests. They are temperate forests, tropical dry forests, and boreal forests. Each type is found in different parts of the world. Different plants and animals live in each forest biome.

Temperate Forests

Temperate forests grow in parts of North America, Europe, and Asia. They get about 20 to 60 inches (51–152 cm) of **precipitation** each year. Precipitation may fall as rain or snow.

The weather in temperate forests changes throughout the year. Summers are warm.

Layers in the Forest

This picture shows the layers that can be found in a forest. Above the forest floor, the layers are made by plants of different heights.

Winters can be very cold. Many plants struggle to survive in low temperatures. Deciduous trees drop their leaves in the fall to prepare for the cold. They grow new leaves in the spring.

This helps them survive. Oaks and maples are deciduous.

Evergreen trees can also be found in temperate forests. These trees keep their leaves year-round. Pine and spruce are evergreen trees. Their leaves are shaped like needles.

Forests on Fire

Wildfires in forests can be helpful. Fire clears out dead wood. By killing some trees, fire makes room for new ones. Black spruce trees grow in boreal forests. They have cones that hold seeds. The cones open only in extreme heat. They need fire to release their seeds.

The miombo woodlands in Africa are an example of a tropical dry forest.

Tropical Dry Forests

Tropical dry forests cover parts of Africa, Latin America, and Asia. Temperatures are warm year-round. About 24 to 60 inches (61–152 cm) of rain falls in tropical dry forests each year. These forests have a wet season and a dry season. Rainfall is more common during the wet season.

Boreal forests have many evergreen trees.

Some trees in tropical dry forests are deciduous. They drop their leaves during the dry season. These trees include teak and mountain ebony.

Boreal Forests

The boreal forest is the largest land biome. Boreal forests grow in the far north. The winters are long and cold. Snow covers the forest floor for most of the year.

Most trees in the boreal forest are evergreen trees. Spruce, fir, and pine trees are common. But a few deciduous trees, such as birch and poplar, grow in the biome.

Further Evidence

Look at the website below. Does it give any new evidence to support Chapter Two?

Temperate Deciduous Forest

abdocorelibrary.com/forest-biomes

Bears are some of the largest animals that live in forest biomes.

CHAPTER 3

A FOREST COMMUNITY

Many plants and animals live in forests. Plants provide food and shelter for forest animals. Animals help carry plant seeds to new places.

Forest Layers

The layers of a forest form different **habitats**. Insects and worms live on the forest floor. They break down waste, such as dead leaves and animal **dung**. They return **nutrients** to the soil.

Deer feed on leaves, seeds, and other plant parts. Rabbits hop along the ground in temperate forests. They eat grasses and flowers.

Forest Recycling

Some living things break down dead plant and animal matter. They are called decomposers. They are important parts of forest biomes. They return nutrients to the soil. Some decomposers are tiny creatures too small to see. Fungi are also decomposers.

Deer have brown coats that help them blend in with the forest.

Predators such as foxes and coyotes hunt animals including rabbits. Coyotes also eat dead animals.

Squirrels live among the tree branches. Birds and bats also make homes or nests in tree branches. Some live in holes in tree trunks. Many birds and bats feed on insects in the canopy.

Spreading Seeds

Animals can help spread plant seeds. Some plants produce tasty fruit with seeds inside.

For example, fig trees grow in tropical dry forests. Animals eat the figs. They later drop fig seeds in their dung in a different area. The new location might be better for the growing plant. The area may be sunnier. There may be fewer plants to compete with. Fewer animals that eat plants may be in the new area.

Birds and bats are common fruit-eaters. Predators can eat fruit too. Raccoon-like animals called coatis eat fruit and small rodents. These predators live in the dry tropical forests of Central and South America. Coatis also live in the southwestern United States.

Large animals can spread seeds very far. Forest elephants might move seeds 63 miles (101 km) from the parent tree. They can have

A coati's long tail helps it balance on tree branches.

a big effect on where different kinds of forest trees grow.

Threats to Forests

Many insects feed on trees. Some eat leaves. Others eat bark. This can hurt trees. They can become sick and die. Unhealthy trees are more likely to be harmed by insects than healthy ones are.

Sometimes insects spread from other parts of the world. For example, the emerald ash borer is an insect native to Asia. These beetles arrived in North America in 2002. They feed on ash trees. They have killed hundreds of millions of ash trees in the United States and Canada.

Humans also harm forest biomes. People cut down trees for wood. They may get rid of forests to use the land for farming. Sometimes the forest

Woodpeckers pick away tree bark to find emerald ash borers to eat.

can recover by itself. Other times people must help the trees regrow.

Plants and animals help make up forest biomes.

Forests biomes are important to the world. Their trees make oxygen that living things need to survive. They cover much of Earth. Forest biomes provide wood and are places to visit and enjoy.

PRIMARY SOURCE

Tony D'Amato is a scientist who studies forests. He talked about the need to protect forests:

> The broadest things we want to maintain are the functions of forest that are so important, so it's clean air . . . it's water filtration, it's bird habitat.

Source: Emma Jacobs. "Foresters Hope 'Assisted Migration' Will Preserve Landscapes as the Climate Changes." *NPR*, 18 May 2022, npr.org. Accessed 15 Sept. 2022.

What's the Big Idea?

Read this quote carefully. What is its main idea? Explain how the main idea is supported by details.

EXPLORE THE BIOME

Many plants and animals help make up forest biomes. Can you identify which parts of this forest biome are plants? Which are animals? Can you find any nonliving parts of the biome?

Glossary

climate
the weather conditions in an area over time

dung
animal poop

habitat
a place where animals and plants are naturally found

nutrients
materials that living things need in order to grow and stay alive

precipitation
liquid or frozen water that falls from the sky, including rain, sleet, and snow

predator
an animal that hunts other animals for food

prey
an animal hunted by other animals for food

Online Resources

To learn more about forest biomes, visit our free resource websites below.

Core Library CONNECTION
FREE! COMMON CORE MULTIMEDIA RESOURCES

Visit **abdocorelibrary.com** or scan this QR code for free Common Core resources for teachers and students, including vetted activities, multimedia, and booklinks, for deeper subject comprehension.

Booklinks NONFICTION NETWORK
FREE! ONLINE NONFICTION RESOURCES

Visit **abdobooklinks.com** or scan this QR code for free additional online weblinks for further learning. These links are routinely monitored and updated to provide the most current information available.

Learn More

French, Jess. *Let's Save Our Planet: Forests.* Ivy Kids, 2020.

Grindler, Sarah. *Forest Magic: A Guidebook for Little Woodland Explorers.* Nimbus, 2021.

Index

acorns, 5–7

bats, 21–22
birds, 21–22, 27
boreal forests, 12, 14, 16–17

deciduous trees, 13–14, 16–17
decomposers, 20

emerald ash borers, 24
evergreen trees, 14, 17

layers, 5, 11–12, 13, 20

precipitation, 12

red-tailed hawks, 7–9
redwood forests, 6

seeds, 14, 19–22
squirrels, 5–9, 21

temperate forests, 12–14, 17, 20
tropical dry forests, 12, 15–16, 22

wildfires, 14

About the Author

Clara MacCarald is a freelance writer with a master's degree in ecology and natural resources. She lives with her family in an off-grid house nestled in the forests of central New York. When not parenting her daughter, she spends her time writing nonfiction books for kids.